Free University of Berlin

The Deutsche Bibliothek holds
a record for this publication in the
Deutsche Nationalbibliografie;
detailed bibliographical data can
be found under http://dnb.ddb.de

Library of Congress Control
Number: 2010942291

©2011, Foster + Partners,
London, and Prestel Verlag,
Munich · London · New York

Prestel Verlag, A Member
of Verlagsgruppe Random
House GmbH

Prestel Verlag
Neumarkter Str. 28
81673 Munich
Germany
Tel   +49 (0)89 4136-0
Fax +49 (0)89 4136-2335
www.prestel.de

Prestel Publishing
900 Broadway, Suite 603
New York NY 10003
USA
Tel   +1 (212) 995-2720
Fax +1 (212) 995-2733

Prestel Publishing Ltd
4 Bloomsbury Place
London
WC1A 2QA
UK
Tel   +44 (020) 7323-5004
Fax +44 (020) 7636-8004
www.prestel.com

ISBN 978-3-7913-4544-4

Free University of Berlin Foster + Partners

Norman Foster
Karl Kiem
Peter Buchanan

PRESTEL
MUNICH · LONDON · NEW YORK

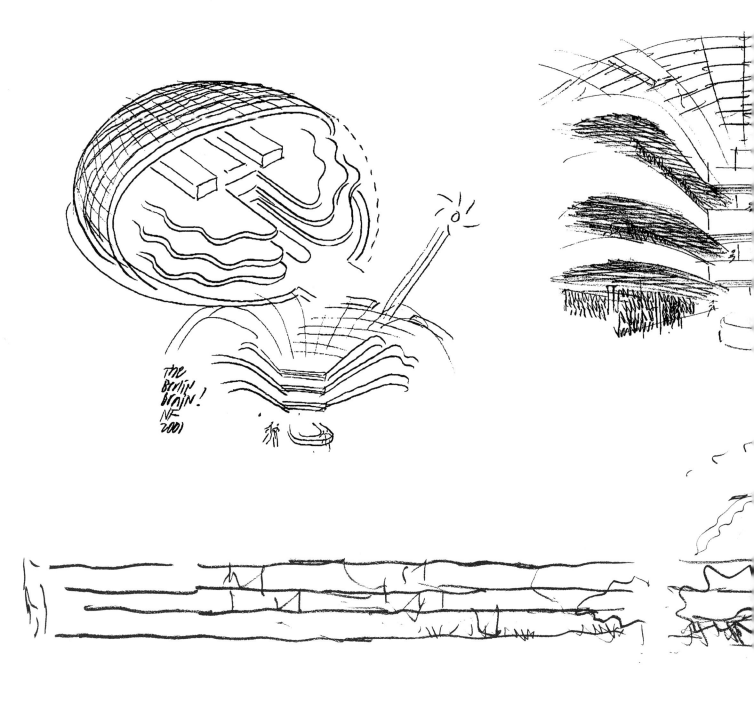

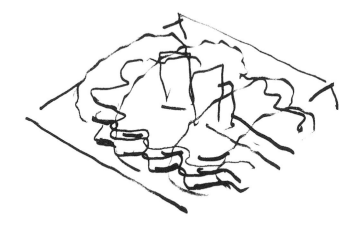

Sketches by Norman Foster made during the early design development of the 'Berlin Brain'.

Overleaf: An aerial view of the Free University, with the silvery form of the library as its new focal point.

Introduction Norman Foster

As a practice we enjoy working in Germany, not least because of the enlightened attitudes that prevail there towards issues such as energy conservation and working with historic buildings. As with the Reichstag, the renewal of the Free University of Berlin allowed us to weave these two themes together. The difference here is that we were working not within the context of a revered national monument, but a Modernist building with its roots in the radicalism and experimentation of the early 1960s.

The Free University occupies a central role in the intellectual history of Berlin, its foundation in 1948 marking the rebirth of liberal education in the city after the war. Today, it is the largest of Berlin's three universities, focused on humanities and social sciences, and is ranked as one of the best in Europe. Our redevelopment of the campus includes the restoration of its Modernist buildings and the design of a new library for the Faculty of Philology.

The University's mat-like campus was designed in 1963 by the architects Candilis-Josic-Woods. When the first buildings were completed in 1973 the project was hailed as a milestone in university design, and would become a model for others around the world.

The facades were designed in collaboration with Jean Prouvé – one of my personal heroes. Prouvé used a proportional system that echoed Le Corbusier's Modulor, and the cladding was designed as a kit of parts that could be demounted and relocated – in effect be almost infinitely flexible. It consisted of modular framing, with flat panel inserts, all made from Corten, or pre-rusted steel. The appearance of these early buildings led to the nickname of 'die Rostlaube' – the 'rust-bucket'.

Over time, however, a number of factors gradually combined to undermine the architects' intentions: the building's potential to be flexible, demountable and extendible was never explored; the poor thermal performance of the cladding created serious environmental problems; and the cladding itself began to decay. When used in the appropriate thickness, Corten steel has self-protecting corrosive characteristics. However, the panelling devised by Prouvé did not stop rusting – the sections were simply too thin. By the 1990s the problem had become so extensive that a radical solution was required. There was no alternative but to replace the cladding entirely.

While the new cladding is essentially faithful to Prouvé's original intentions, we have had to modify some details to meet modern technical and energy standards, which are far more demanding than those that applied when the buildings were designed.

We also decided not to reinstate the cladding in Corten, but instead to recreate it in bronze – a material that should last indefinitely. As it weathers naturally the bronze is slowly gaining the coloration of the Corten, so it is a very sympathetic update. In fact it is now an almost visually exact reproduction of the facades as they were at the time of their creation. We have also planted the flat roofs in order to increase thermal insulation and greatly improve microclimatic conditions.

The new library brings together the holdings of eleven formerly decentralised institute libraries and houses 700,000 books, with 650 reading positions on five floors. In the early search to integrate the library into the fabric of the university 'mat', we rejected the idea of trying to fill an empty courtyard, which would have been problematic in terms of views and natural light. We also rejected the idea of a free-standing building, which would have been too 'aloof'.

Instead we sought to work within the spirit of Candilis-Josic-Woods' building and their strategy for its structural elements to be demounted and relocated. We identified the ideal site for the library, in terms of its wider connection within the University network, and cleared away some parts of the existing fabric to allow us to unite six of the smaller courtyards.

The structural elements we removed were reused to create new rooms elsewhere within the campus.

The design of the library develops ideas that we first explored in the Climatroffice project in the early 1970s with the great American innovator and environmentalist Buckminster Fuller – 'Bucky' as he was affectionately known. Climatroffice was envisaged as a transparent, lightweight dome with its own microclimate, in which nature and the office could interact. Although it was only a theoretical study, it was an exercise with serious potential future application. Climatroffice gave us a clearer focus on many issues: flexibility in use, in the form of multi-function spaces; new means of energy saving; the enclosure of maximum space within the minimum external envelope; the use of lightweight structures; and the value of natural light and ventilation. These are concerns of increasing relevance today.

The Free University project was for us a quest for the ideal library. We realised that students would spend hundreds of hours working there during the course of their studies and we wanted to provide them with the best possible environment. But what would be the best conditions in which to work? Would you want to see into the courtyard; how could we get light in; should there be large areas of glass; if we used diffused light and had only glimpses of the courtyard, would that be better; if you were sitting reading or working, should you face other people, or should you look outwards to get the right level of focus and privacy? The scale and height of the building were also critical considerations. The existing university buildings are predominantly of two storeys and the suburb of Dahlem in which it stands is low-rise and residential, so we had to respect that and ensure that the library would not be too dominant a presence.

We concluded that the library should be user friendly and intuitive. I have characterised it as being an analogue building in a digital age: it is a very natural diagram – everything is where it wants to be. The bookstacks are located in the centre of each floor, where light levels are lower – the perfect environment for books – and the reading desks are arranged around the perimeter, where you have daylight and privacy and are within easy reach of the stacks.

The edges of the floors follow serpentine curves, which have the effect of lengthening the edge condition and maximising desk space, and the profile of each floor swells or recedes with respect to the one above it, creating a continuous pattern of generous, light-filled spaces in which to work.

Environmentally, we sought to combine active and passive technologies to maximum advantage. That required us to think holistically in order to form a cohesive relationship between the solar path, the natural ventilation system and the configuration of the external skin.

A modified hemisphere in form, the library is inserted into the mat so that it plugs into the University's circulation 'streets' at two strategic points. In order to reduce its perceived height, the building is dug down one floor into the courtyard. The 'cut' around the perimeter also corresponds with the external flaps that form part of the natural ventilation scheme. Fresh air is fed into a plenum beneath the basement floor and rises naturally through the floor slab above and through ventilation shafts to the upper floors.

The structural system we selected is a space frame with a radial geometry, made by the German company MERO. This system proved extremely effective in contouring the enclosure. Externally, the frame is clad in aluminium panels, punctuated by ventilation flaps and glazed openings. Internally, a translucent glass-fibre membrane catches the daylight and diffuses it so that there is a very even distribution of light. This helps to create a visually calm atmosphere, which is appropriate in a library. As a counterpoint, scattered window openings create changing patterns of light and shade, and offer momentary views of the sky and glimpses of sunlight.

The depth of the MERO structure has the effect of creating a wide cavity between the building's inner and outer skins. We harnessed this cavity to create a 'solar engine' to drive the ventilation system. Fresh air is drawn in at low level, through the flaps in the outer skin, circulated up through the cavity and vents in the inner skin, and finally vented at the top of the building. In a playful allusion to the use of colour in the original campus, we painted the elements of the MERO space frame yellow, which has the effect of making it legible and emphasising the cavity between the two skins. It is also a literally sunny colour.

In contrast to the structural envelope, which is essentially 'light', the inner structure – the floors and supporting columns – is deliberately heavy, built of reinforced concrete. One visitor described the building as 'a battleship inside an airship' which I think is very apt. The thermal mass of this exposed concrete structure is exploited and the floors have embedded water pipes that can provide heating or cooling.

When the internal temperature is within the range from +16 to +24 degrees Celsius, cooling is provided by running chilled water through the floors and the natural ventilation system is in operation. Only very occasionally, on the hottest summer days – roughly eight to ten times a year – is mechanical cooling required. This is provided by the University's existing compression coolers. There is no need for full air conditioning or humidity control.

When temperatures are in the range from +8 to +16 degrees Celsius, heating is provided by running hot water through the pipes in the floors. Meanwhile, natural ventilation still operates for most of the time. When the internal temperature falls below +8 degrees Celsius, additional heating is provided by the University's district heating system. In this event, the flaps in the outer skin remain closed and the warm air in the cavity acts as thermal buffer. The inner skin flaps stay open to extract waste air, which is drawn through a heat-recovery system. All these components are coordinated by an electronic building management system. The net effect is a building that remarkably uses 35 per cent less energy than any of the other new university libraries recently constructed in Berlin.

As a footnote, I was pleased to discover, before it was even completed, that the library's cranial form had earned it an affectionate nickname of its own – 'the Berlin Brain' – christened appropriately by the academic community it serves.

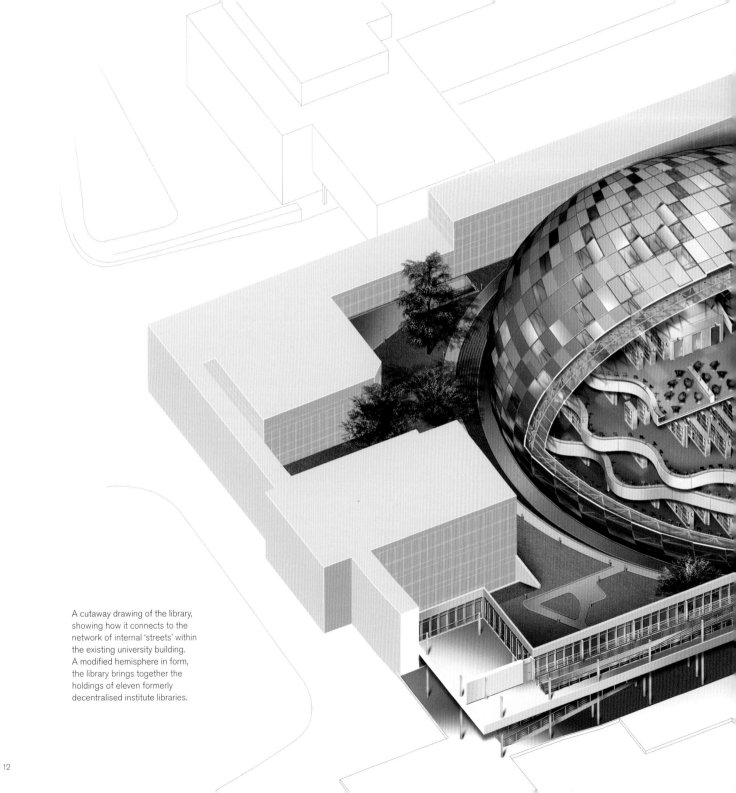

A cutaway drawing of the library, showing how it connects to the network of internal 'streets' within the existing university building. A modified hemisphere in form, the library brings together the holdings of eleven formerly decentralised institute libraries.

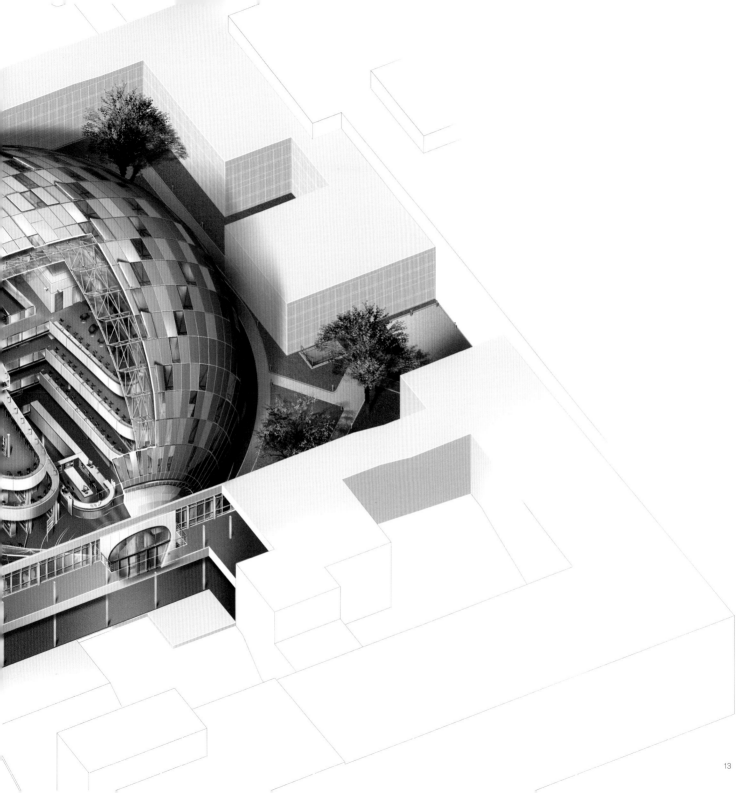

Die Rostlaube Karl Kiem

In August 1963 work began in Candilis-Josic-Woods' studio in Paris on the competition design for the Free University of Berlin. Leading the project was Shadrach Woods (1923-1973). An American, he had studied mechanical engineering in New York, and literature in Dublin, before going to study under Le Corbusier in Paris in 1948. A true intellectual, he was one of the key members of Team X, and taught at Harvard and Yale as well as other academic institutions. The second key figure was Manfred Schiedhelm, a German, who graduated from Darmstadt in 1958 and subsequently went to Paris where he worked for Marcel Lods. He moved to Candilis-Josic-Woods in 1962 and later became a partner in the practice.

By 1963 Candilis-Josic-Woods had an excellent reputation all over the world. The two partners Georges Candilis and Shadrach Woods met in Le Corbusier's office, where they worked together on the building of the Unité d'Habitation in Marseilles. The practice's reputation was mainly founded on large urban development projects, but its profile also benefited from the leading roles played by Candilis and Woods in Team X, which had succeeded CIAM and greatly influenced architectural discourse in the 1960s.

Staff in the practice were drawn from international backgrounds. Candilis was a Greek, born in Uzbekistan, and Alexis Josic was a Serb from Yugoslavia. Those involved in the latter phase of building the Free University included, in addition to Schiedhelm, the Englishman Jonathan Greig, the Italian Armando Barp, the Pole Jacek Damniecky and the Japanese woman Noriko Hajashi.

This international orientation meant that the office was particularly well informed about university building, an area of expertise it consolidated in the 1950s, on a global scale. Whereas in Europe after the Second World War it was mainly the existing universities that were being extended, in the so-called second and third world a whole range of large-scale university complexes were being established. These were typically designed according to the principles of the 'Ville Radieuse' propounded by Le Corbusier, with each faculty occupying its own discrete building.

The move away from this principle began with the University of Baghdad, which was based on a design by Walter Gropius and The Architects' Collaborative (after 1959). Here the university was designed around the centralised timetable principle, in which individual building units were abandoned in favour of compact building structures that could be used in a flexible way. In principle, all the classrooms were intended to be used by every faculty, which meant that they needed

Above: An aerial view of the first
phase of Candilis-Josic-Woods'
larger scheme for the Free
University of Berlin – known
as 'die Rostlaube' – in 1974.

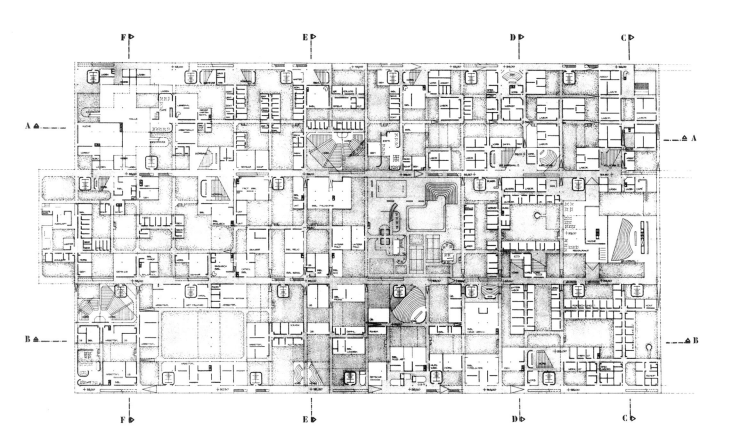

Above: Candilis-Josic-Woods' competition plan for the campus, only a small part of which was ever built. Within the grid, longitudinal 'streets' are identified with letters, intersected by perpendicular 'cross-streets' represented by numerals. The architects began the lettering in the middle of the alphabet – with streets J, K and L – and cross-streets from 28 to 33, envisaging this as a fragment of a much larger university 'mat'.

Left: Members of the Candilis-Josic-Woods team photographed with the Free University of Berlin competition model outside the studio on Rue Dauphine in Paris. From left: Giorgio Cicercia, model maker Armando Barp, Jonathan ...dhelm.

http://www.pbclibrary.org

Check your account at.

Item Due: 11/1/2015

...580

...093 FRE

Title: Free University, Berlin

Checkout Date: 06/09/2015
001-744-2301
FORT MYERS-REGIONAL

LEE COUNTY LIBRARY

...dents ...ak ...tion ...rder ...n a ...:ame ...d ...uld ...sity s, ...ut as ...s as ...d by ...and ...idual ...contact ...ove ...al separation between arts and natural sciences. This means that the Free University can be regarded conceptually not only as a university building but also as an ideal town.

The rejection of the 'matchbox style' of the CIAM establishment was also one of the central identifying ideas of Team X. Their theory was much closer to the space-time concepts of the 1920s. With the design for the Free University the corresponding idea of 'four-dimensionality' of architecture was taken a long way forward. The great significance of the 'movement' in this structure is expressed particularly through the location of the system of main 'streets', which run parallel to each other at a distance of 65.63 metres. These are connected to the surrounding road network and have good residential features.

The other aspects of four-dimensionality – the possibility that the building structure can grow and change over time to allow the interior and exterior to merge – were incorporated to a remarkable degree in the design. At the same time, the design essentially followed Le Corbusier's 'Five Points of a New Architecture'. Corbusier's influence is further manifested in the use of the Modulor as a measuring system, the 'interplay of fillings' as a basis for the composition of facade panels and the horizontal sunshade, or brise-soleil, as originally proposed but not finally incorporated. We can detect further Corbusian influences in the Free University's subtle path network, the use of ramps and the finely differentiated design

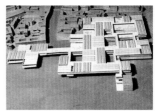

of the courtyards; here the empathy for people moving around and through the building – and the corresponding *promenade architecturale* – plays a particularly important role. The fact that Le Corbusier, in his design for the Venice Hospital (1964), was in turn inspired by the design for the Free University of Berlin shows how complex the influence was on both sides.

With other features of the Free University the different influences are piled on top of each other. This is why in the 1960s the terms 'growth' and 'change' took on such an important role in avant-garde architectural discourse. We can identify Corbusier and Marcel Lods as the important personalities in whose architectural ethos the terms 'growth' and 'change' also played an important role and in turn had a direct influence on Woods and Schiedhelm. The Maison du Peuple in Clichy, a building that offered true flexibility of use, which Marcel Lods built together with his partner at that time, Eugène Beaudouin, in cooperation with Jean Prouvé and Vladimir Bodiansky, can likewise be seen as a forerunner to the Free University.

Equally it also reflects the influence of older architecture. The universal gridded street network is particularly important in this connection, something which Woods and Schiedhelm illustrated in their competition submission using examples from, among others, the cities of Milet, Montpazier, Mannheim and Manhattan. Schiedhelm has even said that the medieval university colleges with their secluded courtyards, such as those in Oxford and Cambridge, had an influence on the design.

Amongst other early models for the Free University, traditional North African architecture also plays a role. The influence was passed on in this case via Woods, who worked for Le Corbusier's subsidiary ATBAT-Afrique together with Candilis for five years from 1951. During this time he gained day-to-day experience of Arabic building forms in Algeria and Morocco. In fact, Woods so closely identified with the French-North African culture in Morocco that he threw off his customary image – based on the American film star Alan Ladd – and started dressing like Albert Camus.

With this in mind, Candilis' statement that the 'streets' of the Free University had their origin in the bazaars of North African cities and in particular the souks of Marrakech, seems entirely plausible. Moreover, one is reminded of the model of the old Arab city when one looks at other features of the design, such as the flat labyrinthine structure, the fact that all the rooms face on to courtyards, and the almost total abandonment of architectural

Above left: Aldo van Eyck's Children's Home, Amsterdam (1955-1960). A celebrated 'web structure' scheme of the period, it immediately predates the Free University competition and was a point of reference for Candilis-Josic-Woods.

Above right: A detail of Le Corbusier's unrealised Venice Hospital (1964-1965). The 'mat' project par excellence, it can be seen to draw on ideas developed in the Free University.

This scheme is an attempt to discover structuring principles which might be applicable to the organization of physical environment. The university is considered as a place and a tool.
Candilis-Josic-Woods' statement for the competition project, 1963

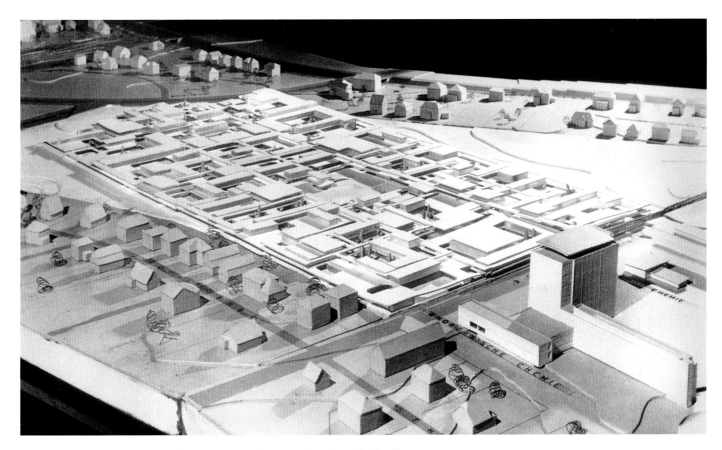

Left: Candilis-Josic-Woods used diagrams to explain how the grid module would allow mobility and access to locations where people would cluster – such as lecture halls or seminar rooms.

Above: A model of Candilis-Josic-Woods' competition scheme for the Free University. A horizontal 'mat' of streets and boulevards is repeated in various configurations at different levels, with the floors connected by ramps and stairs. This dense arrangement is punctuated by courtyards, which provide social spaces.

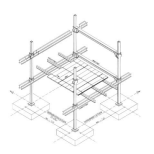

representation. It is also possible that Corten steel was chosen for the facades because its colour reminded Woods of the clay buildings in North Africa.

In terms of literature that influenced the design, Woods mentions the book *Community and Privacy* by Serge Chermayeff and Christopher Alexander, published in 1963. (A book, incidentally, with which Norman Foster is intimately familiar, having been invited by his tutor, Chermayeff, to review it in draft). Chermayeff and Alexander express a clear dislike of suburban development forms and the car as the main mode of transport, which we can see reflected in the design of the Free University.

Another intellectual mentor was Louis Kahn. With its ability to grow and to form an internal unity in each stage, and in the abandonment of axes and symmetries, the Free University reveals similarities with Kahn's work. Indeed, Woods directly incorporated Kahn's distinction between 'servant' and 'served' zones into his description of the project.

The cultural climate in Paris in the early 1960s can also be said to have had a certain influence. At that time, a new highly confident generation was emerging in a society characterised among other things by sustained economic growth, full employment and rapid developments in mobility and the media. In art, there

Left and above: Designed to facilitate 'growth' and 'change' and thus be almost infinitely flexible, Jean Prouvé's so-called 'stool' construction system comprised prefabricated concrete floor slabs, steel beams and composite steel and concrete columns.

This demountable system could be 'clipped' together in numerous configurations. The construction process was entirely industrialised, the building site organised 'like a car factory'.

was a tendency to question conventional forms in a radical way. People were trying to merge works of art and life itself: for example, in the form of a 'happening'. Woods and Schiedhelm at that time were particularly interested in the machine-like movable sculptures of Jean Tinguely and the Free Jazz of Ornette Coleman. With the design of the Free University they tried to give architectural expression to this spirit.

In view of this wide spectrum of influences, Woods and Schiedhelm clearly managed to create an individual design for the Free University. In the context of the surrounding villas they succeeded in creating a small-scaled and harmoniously proportioned building, which nonetheless makes no secret of its size and function. A flexible structure, which encouraged interaction and communication, it contrasted with the rigid, stuffy and gloomy university buildings they themselves had experienced.

A key figure in the detailed design of the building was the construction pioneer Jean Prouvé. It was Prouvé who emphasised the necessity of industrial manufacture and a corresponding architectural expression within the building's structure. Woods was also a vigorous defender of industrialised building techniques. He agreed with Prouvé that the building site should be organised 'like a car factory' and he

sought his cooperation wherever possible. The load-bearing structure that Prouvé developed for the Free University is known as the *système tabouret* [stool system]. The description derives from the stool-like structure, which has a square frame made of double 'T' sections mounted on four round supports and has rigid corners. The structure is covered with a three-dimensional framework that allows the position of the supports to be varied. This design originated from the engineer Léon Pétroff and owes its development to computers, which could be applied to statistical calculation after 1960.

The load-bearing system developed by Prouvé consists of a pillar/panel construction. This featured in his work for the first time in 1938 with the Maison du Peuple in Clichy and then developed through numerous variations. Here the pillars were separated from the shell construction using upper and lower braces. In the case of the exterior walls the load-bearing 'U' section was set in front of the facade. For the interior walls it was mounted in the form of a square on each side using a cover rail and was designed to be tensioned above and below between foot and ceiling rails. Wall elements such as panels, windows and doors were planned in the same forms and dimensions for both the facades and the partition walls.

Above left: A storey-height cladding panel is mounted within the facade framework.

Above right: A typical faculty office in the newly completed building. The light fittings were specially designed, but budgetary constraints meant that the demountable partitioning system was selected 'off the peg'.

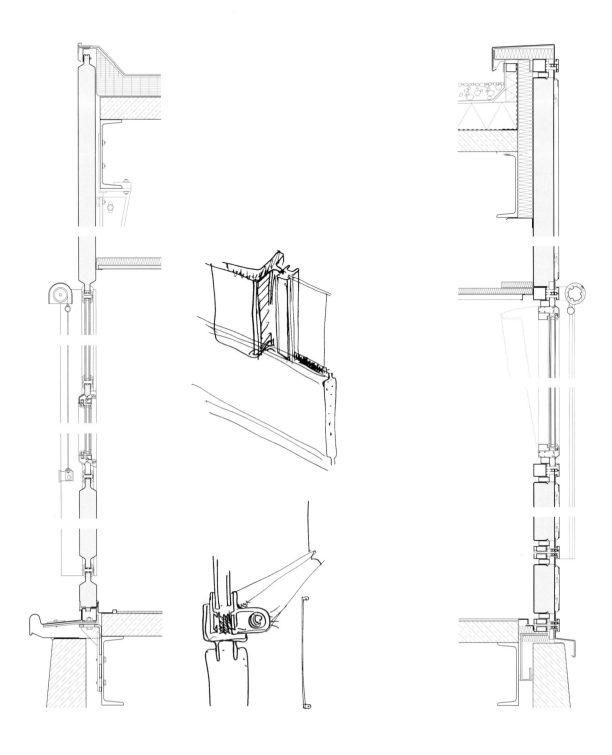

Right: 'Before' and 'after' details of the cladding. Jean Prouvé's Corten steel system is on the left and the replacement bronze system on the right.

In building the Free University, however, the architects gradually had to accept that certain sensitive features of the concept would have to be left out. Early on, virtually all the movable parts were omitted in order to save costs. Later the load-bearing structure developed by Prouvé was abandoned in favour of a more conventional solution, but one that offered fewer conversion possibilities.

When it came to the contract to build the facades Prouvé and his company CIMT were restricted to designing and planning the work, whereas the manufacture and assembly was assigned to a small Berlin-based steel window company. The interior wall system designed by Prouvé was replaced by an existing proprietary product.

Problems with the facade delayed the completion of the building for nearly three years. In the first phase of the work, difficulties with water penetration led the two companies involved to focus more energy on apportioning blame than on construction. For the second phase of the work, the Dortmund-based company C H Jucho was commissioned to rework the facade construction, to carry out the necessary repair work and complete the first phase of building, and to manufacture the facade for the second phase. However, after the building opened in 1971, it was

discovered that the facade as reworked by Jucho was still not entirely waterproof.

It has never been possible to explain the causes for the leaks. The share of this problem that can be attributed to Prouvé may derive from a certain willingness to take risks, born out of a desire to remain at the peak of technological development and to vary even tried and tested solutions to a large extent. Furthermore, the experiment in which the building site was organised like a factory ultimately had an adverse effect on the quality of construction. Poor management was another factor. The files also show that there was a clash between different national mentalities. We can only speculate as to what extent the project may also have been damaged by anti avant-garde sentiment.

Other problems can be attributed to the fact that, at the time the Free University was built, European architects and contractors did not have enough expertise in working with Corten steel. It was discovered, for example, that particles of rust had eaten into the glass surfaces as a result of rainwater run-off – a problem that nobody had anticipated. More serious was the fact that, contrary to assurances given by the industry, in the damp Berlin climate the external rust layer was not able to protect the Corten steel for very long. Shortly after the building opened it became clear

Opposite: Jean Prouvé's sketches and a detailed section through original cladding system (left) with the corresponding section through the new cladding (right). Prouvé's system failed on numerous counts – technical and environmental. The new cladding conforms to current building codes, which are far more demanding than those in force at the time the building was constructed. Although essentially faithful to Prouvé's design intentions, the new cladding is dimensionally deeper and the parapet slightly higher.

A detail of the new bronze
cladding system; over time,
the brightness of the bronze
dulls naturally to a 'rusty' brown
not dissimilar to the original
Corten steel.

The cladding was designed using Corb's Modulor. We decided to use that too, though we had to adjust the vertical height of the panels because of the greater roof build-up to meet new regulations. We tried to preserve the original detailing as far as possible.
David Nelson, of Foster + Partners, 2010

that at some point in the future the whole facade would be eaten away by rust. To avoid such a problem, thicker panels should have been used, but few outside the steel industry were aware of this at the time.

Candilis-Josic-Woods was also partly responsible for other problems with the building. For example, it turned out that the dark colour of the facade meant that the rooms overheated in the summer months. Readings showed that with an external temperature of 32 degrees Celcius and non-activated sun protection, the temperature inside south-facing areas of the building would typically reach 44 to 45 degrees.

The architects' rather astonishing suggestion that people should not open the windows in the summer due to the very overheated layer of air situated very close to the building, was not communicated to the users, but it is hard to imagine that it would have been taken seriously in any case. Instead the University asked for an air-conditioning system to be installed. Finally the University management decided to move employees who were required to sit at their desks all day to cooler parts of the building. Another problem, resulting from leaks in the flat roofs, was that water repeatedly came into the building, rendering the underfloor sockets unusable.

During the first few years of the Free University's life, as these problems began to come to light, articles attacking 'die Rostlaube' – the 'rust-bucket' – started to appear in the West Berlin and national press. Those who used the building, however, increasingly came to recognise its qualities, learning to appreciate the benefits it had to offer and even developing a sort of pride in being associated with a very special building. Furthermore, as soon as the teaching got under way, some of the friendly and varied personal interaction that the architects had envisaged started to develop in the corridors, courtyards and terraces.

After barely three decades of use, in 1997 a limited competition was staged to find an architect for the building's radical refurbishment, which Foster + Partners won. It took courage and imagination to conceive how the building's facade – by then severely decayed – could be transformed, while remaining faithful to the system developed by Jean Prouvé. Indeed, Foster was the only architect to demonstrate a real understanding of the challenges that refurbishing the building presented. Although Corten steel – which over time had fallen into disrepute and even been removed from building construction textbooks – is now being used for some contemporary avant-garde buildings, it was ruled out for this project.

Above left: A typical classroom in the newly refurbished building. The original colour scheme has been retained and original fixtures and fittings cleaned and re-used.

Above right: The demountable partitioning panels were stripped and repainted and the carpet recreated by the manufacturer to the exact specification and colour of the original.

It would not have provided the material strengths necessary to maintain the slender sections and fine detail of Prouvé's cladding system. Instead the new facade is detailed in bronze, which – as it patinates with age – emulates the colour tones of the original.

If Foster has taken a step into the past with the reworking of the facade and the general refurbishment of the building's interiors, he has at the same time made considerable progress in terms of the new library that he has placed within the web of the University complex. Shadrach Woods would surely have had nothing against such an addition. Its installation has, for the first time, properly exploited the structural flexibility of the Free University load-bearing structure, just as Woods intended.

The Free University has been fortunate. The overall reworking and additions to its structural substance by Foster + Partners have given the building a design that not only respects its extraordinary significance in the history of modern architecture but at the same time develops these qualities further. It means that the architects' original dream, of designing a building to promote teaching and learning in flat hierarchies and open, flexible structures whilst providing opportunities for friendly and creative contact, can finally become a functioning structural reality.

Above: Looking into the two lecture theatres. The approach in restoring these spaces was to use the lightest possible touch; they are seen now essentially as they were when first completed.

Above: The principal entrance to the 'Rostlaube' buildings from Malteserstrasse, following the refurbishment of the campus.

Right: A detail of the new cladding on a courtyard facade; the sun blinds are an integral part of the cladding system and follow in the spirit of the originals.

Particularly now, in its pristine restored glory, the building shows a wonderfully fresh and thoughtful approach to individual questions of design. Christian Brensing, *The Architects' Journal*, 15 September 2005

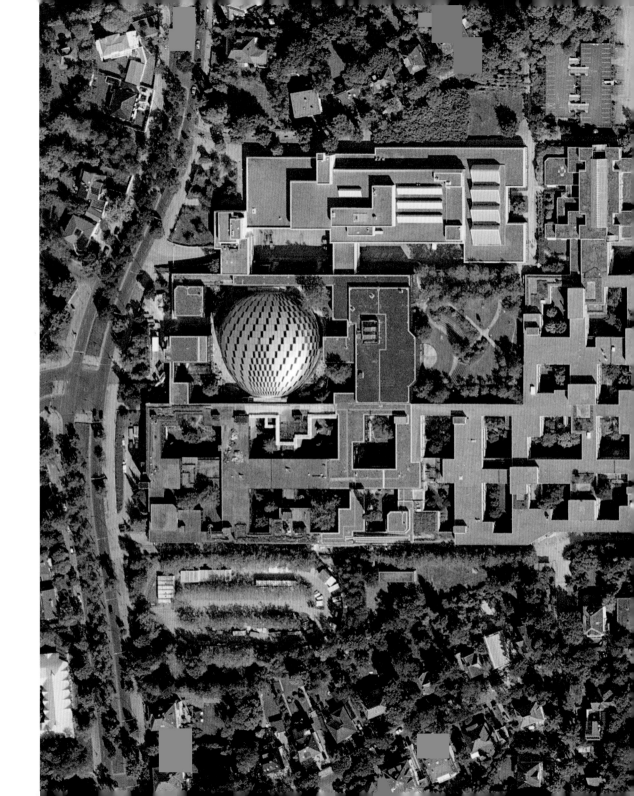

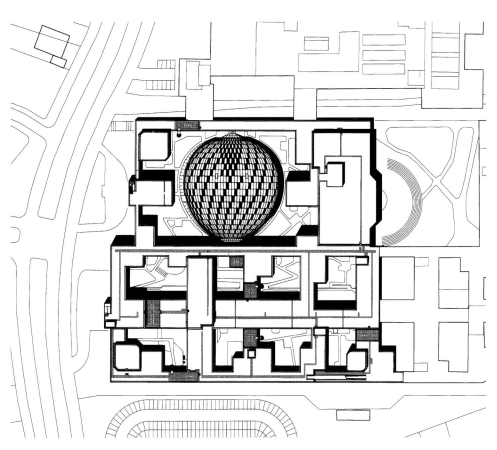

Left: An aerial view of the Free
University of Berlin campus.
Six of the University's courtyards
have been united to form the
site of a new library for the
Faculty of Philology.

Above: Site plan, showing the
new library located within the
'Rostlaube' – the first phase
of Candilis-Josic-Woods'
Free University campus.

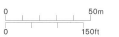

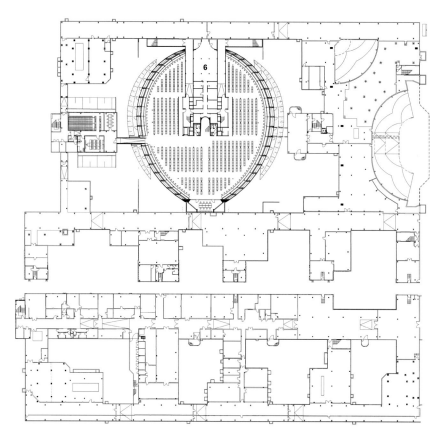

Left: Lower-ground floor plan.

Right: Ground floor plan.

1 side entrance
2 library administration
3 main entrance
4 lecture hall
5 L street
6 philological library
7 K street
8 philological institutes
9 J street
10 main auditorium
11 link to adjoining buildings

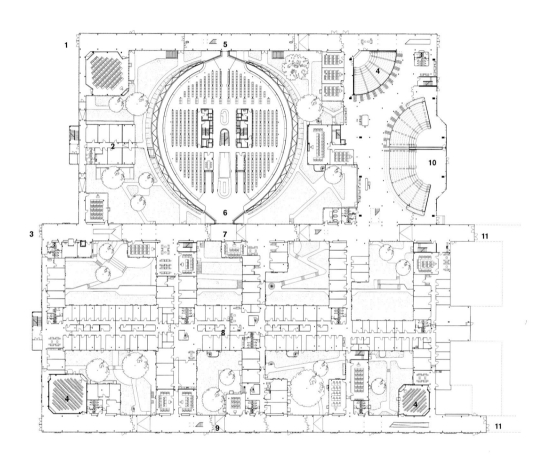

The library building, seen
from one of the ground-
floor classrooms in the
philological institute.

Foster's library offers a wealth of different perspectives, the routes that all readers must use are short, visual relationships to others are opened up, and the building presents itself as a mediator between past and future.
Claus Käpplinger, *Architektur Aktuell*, December 2005

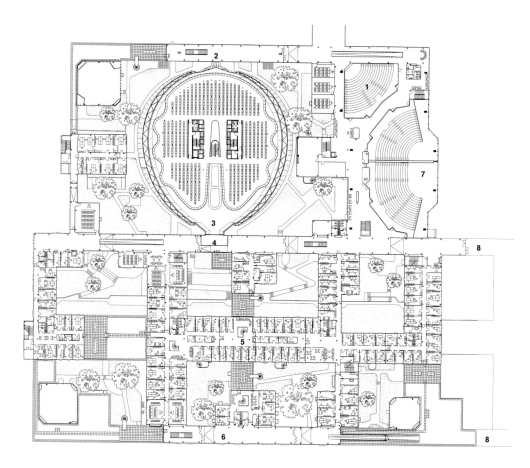

Left: First floor plan.

Right: Second floor plan.

1 lecture hall
2 L street
3 philological library
4 K street
5 philological institutes
6 J street
7 main auditorium
8 link to adjoining buildings

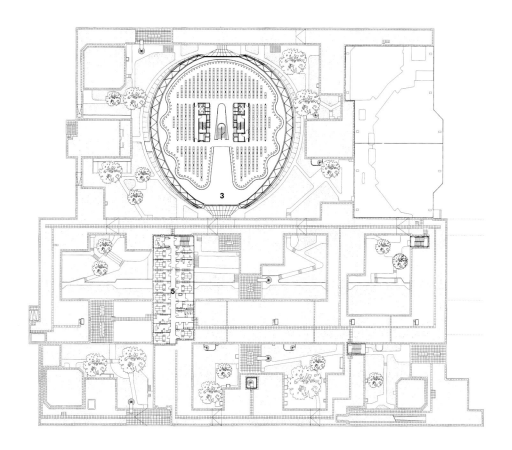

The library comes as one of those wonderful surprises you might find just beyond a lively piazza in some Tuscan hill town … Inside it turns out to be a comfortable and engaging place to study. Clifford A Pearson, *Architectural Record*, November 2006

The silvery form of the library, glimpsed here from one of the second-floor rooms in the philological institute.

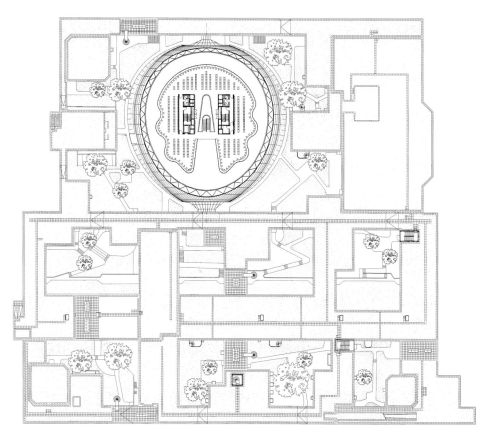

Above: Third floor plan,
corresponding with roof level
of the institute buildings.

Right: Roof plan of the library.

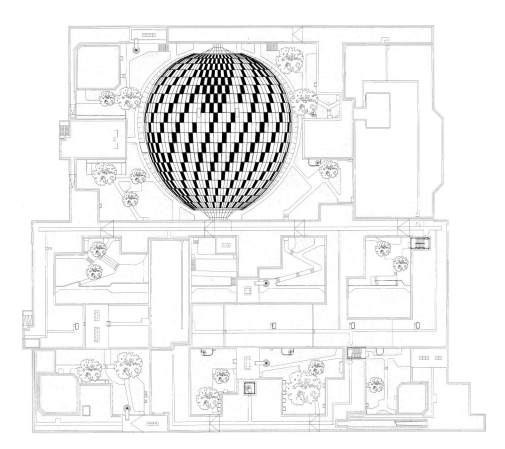

Overleaf: Looking from the
adjacent courtyard into the
library entrance on K street.

The Berlin Brain Peter Buchanan

For Foster + Partners, to refurbish the original buildings and build a new library for the Free University of Berlin was, metaphorically speaking, to revisit the soil in which Norman Foster's early work is rooted and from which it grew. The aesthetic might be very different – so much so that Foster's architecture might seem a reaction against buildings such as the Free University – but the design of the university, which was radical and experimental in its time, was shaped by concepts strikingly similar to those that inform Foster's architecture. In particular, both are concerned with providing flexibility for growth and change, in part by using a kit of purpose-made components that exploits the latest technology.

Though largely forgotten today, the Free University was one of the seminal projects of the mid-twentieth century. Candilis-Josic-Woods' competition-winning design of 1963 was widely published and discussed well before its partial realisation began. Georges Candilis and Shadrach Woods were key members of Team X. The design marked a climactic extreme in a significant strand of Team X's design explorations, showing clearly how far it had departed from the conventions of CIAM and the Athens Charter.

Instead of buildings standing free in space and remote from roads, you find buildings and circulation routes connected in branching and web-like patterns, such as in the Smithsons' Golden Lane Housing (1952) project or Candilis-Josic-Woods' Toulouse-le-Mirail urban plan (1961-71). The Free University takes this approach to its ultimate as a low-rise 'mat' with a warp and weft of primary and secondary circulation routes between which are classrooms and courtyards. This was the heyday of interdisciplinary studies and here the boundaries between faculties disappeared as they melted into one another.

Constant restructuring was anticipated and facilitated by the ease of rearranging spaces, while the grid of circulation spaces and the green courtyards adjacent to them promoted educative and community-forging social interaction. Such a design is particularly apt to the Free University, which remains committed to interdisciplinary studies and research, while the emphasis on freedom and flux, like the University's name, suggested a calculated contrast with Communist constraints.

The Free University is yet another of those twentieth-century designs based on radical concepts that have proved problematic. Yet, it could also be argued, it was never fully tested because only a small proportion was realised. As discussed in the preceding essay, the problems were both technical and social.

Right: The external skin of the library emulates the tensile properties of a water droplet.

Chief among the technical failings was the cladding. Designed with Jean Prouvé, the first phase was clad in Corten steel, then a largely untried material in Europe. Unfortunately, in the slender sections specified by Prouvé, the rusty patination that was supposed to protect the steel never did so and the panels and mullions began to corrode. Compounding problems of decay, the cladding panels were poorly insulated, so that interiors were freezing in winter and unbearably hot in summer; and as was typical of the period, asbestos was used extensively in construction and would later have to be removed.

Many of the problems with this system were detected early on, and so the second phase was clad in silvery aluminium that contrasted starkly with the dark, matt surfaces of the Corten. Inevitably the two phases acquired nicknames that translate as the 'rust bucket' and the 'silver bucket'.

Major social problems also emerged. These can be traced to the lack of differentiation between faculties and departments and the porosity of the plan. People could move freely through all parts of the building, but they could disappear equally easily. This resulted in disorientation, especially amongst new students, and vulnerability to various sorts of crime, including vandalism.

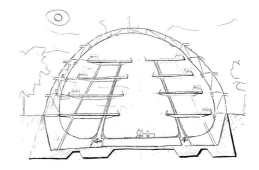

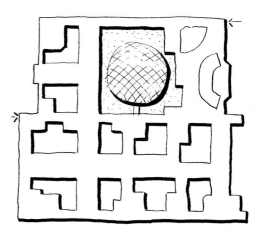

Right above: An early sketch by Stefan Behling, setting out ideas for the library's natural ventilation system.

Right below: A drawing by David Nelson exploring how the oval form of the library might be inserted into the orthogonal 'mat' of the university buildings.

Above and right: These early
study models – just two of twenty
made by the team – begin to
explore how five storeys could be
contained within as shallow a
form as possible. The sectional
organisation follows an elemental
logic: the books are placed in
the heart of the space – away
from the light – where they
can be stored in a constant
environment; and the reading
desks gravitate towards the light,
lining the perimeter of each floor.

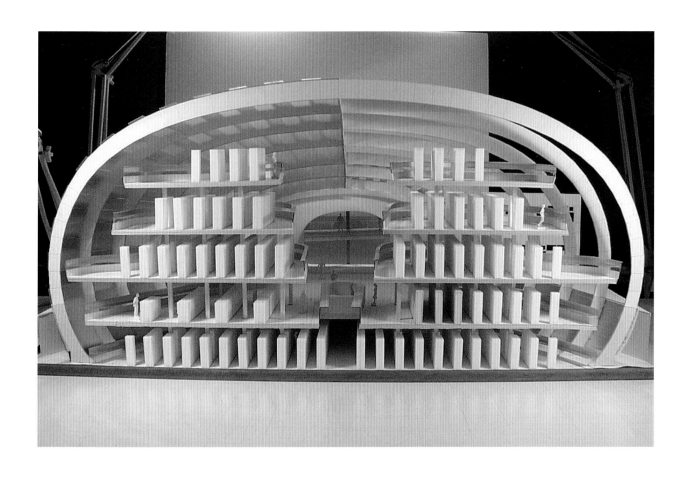

Right: The Climatroffice – a
theoretical study into new forms
of office building, undertaken
with Buckminster Fuller (1971).

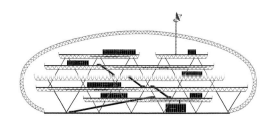

Besides these failings, there was another potent
reason the original scheme was never completed.
The university lies in the middle-class suburb of
Dahlem – chosen because distinguished scientific
research institutes, botanic gardens and museums
were already located there – whose residents resisted
further incursions on their salubrious setting. To
expand, some faculties acquired nearby villas, leading
to fragmentation and dispersal – the antithesis of
the original concept. The various departments of
the philology (language studies) faculty, for example,
each had their own libraries spread between
seven villas.

In 1997 an invited competition asked for proposals
as to how to refurbish the original 'rust bucket'
buildings and provide a single philology library. The
jury included Alexis Josic, the last living member of
the original architectural partnership. Foster + Partners,
who already had a Berlin office then busy with the
Reichstag, won the competition: in large part because
of the respect with which Foster proposed to treat the
original buildings, refurbishing and recycling as much
of the fabric as possible, or replacing components with
new ones closely matching the originals. The Foster
team offered alternative locations for the library, one
on an existing car park adjacent the original buildings
and the other concealed in a courtyard created by
selectively removing and relocating some parts
of the existing building. The jury and university
overwhelmingly endorsed the latter solution.

Refurbishing the 'rust bucket' would present a
number of technical challenges, not least the fact that
all new construction had to conform to much more
stringent building codes than did the original. Prouvé's
cladding was dimensioned according to Le Corbusier's
Modulor, with panels of differing width and transoms
at differing heights giving the syncopated rhythms and
jittery animation with which Le Corbusier enlivened his
buildings. Here the panels meet behind projecting
vertical rails to give further articulation; and as well as
solid and glazed sections there are boxy projections
that form niches for shelves on the inside. Foster
decided to follow this pattern as closely as possible
in a durable material that would be similar in colour
to Corten and would patinate to a similar dark colour
with a soft and warm haptic quality. Eventually a form
of bronze, in this case a mixture of copper and pewter,
was found that met the criteria yet cost only 10 per
cent more than aluminium. However, to conform to
the modern building regulations, the panels are thicker
than the original, and the horizontal strip facing floors
and roof somewhat deeper, so the proportions are

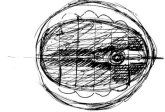

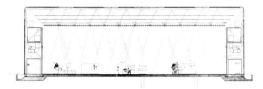

Left: Cross-section through
the Sainsbury Centre for Visual
Arts (1974-1978); there are
strong links between this
building, with its deep double
skin, and the design of the
Free University library.

not an exact match, though only those to whom
it is pointed out will notice.

Eliminating the asbestos (a process that began
in 1999) required removing the original ceilings and
replacing them with similar acoustic tiles. Some original
light fittings have been refurbished and reused, but
elsewhere there are new light fittings. The original
partitioning system has been refurbished and, as
before, the carpet continues under the panels to
facilitate ease of rearrangement. The original carpet,
which extends throughout the building with changes
of colour to facilitate orientation, was heavily worn.
But the manufacturer still had samples so an identical
carpet has been woven and relaid. Measures have also
been taken to remedy the problems with orientation
and vulnerability to crime. The central of the three
longitudinal corridor 'streets' has been made the
dominant one, off which each faculty now has a clearly
defined front entrance controlled by a reception desk.
The area occupied by each faculty is better defined
too, with less overlapping in section than before. All
this work was finally competed in 2007, some time
after the completion of the philology library in 2005,
its construction having begun in 2001.

The main entrance to the new philology library
lies on the now dominant central corridor. Space

for the library was freed up by amalgamating six
small courtyards and reusing components from the
dismantled intervening construction to replace the lost
accommodation in the form of a third floor over some
parts of the building. To best use the courtyard space
the library was always to have been on a number of
levels, including a basement, yet not rise high enough
to be visible from outside the university. Originally
the library was to be rectangular in plan and more or
less filled the courtyard. But this proved problematic,
providing no outlook for the library and robbing those
parts of the existing building adjacent the courtyard
of light as well as views.

As design progressed the corners of the volume
were gradually eroded, so creating space in the
corners of the courtyard for light and views. Eventually
an ovoid plan was settled on, with a basement and
three floors above a ground floor, which measures
64 metres long by 55 metres wide. In total, the
resulting floor area is 6,290 square metres, housing
650 reading places and 700,000 books, all snugly
enveloped by a flattened dome-like roof that is
19 metres high externally.

This roof form brought several advantages. It could
admit natural light while enclosing a maximum volume
with minimal area of enclosure. This latter was crucial

Far left: The Autonomous
House, a project Norman Foster
developed with Buckminster
Fuller (1983); the house's
double skin becomes a
climate-modifying device.

Left: A sketch by David Nelson
in which the double skin and
the serpentine form of the
library floors begin to appear.

as the budget was extremely tight: construction cost €20million, 10 per cent less per square metre than the conventionally constructed TU Berlin Bibliothek, built at the same time. Running costs were also to be reduced by exploiting natural light and ventilation to achieve energy efficiencies. The domed roof plays a key role here too, particularly the ventilated cavity between the panelled outer skin and the translucent fabric ceiling. However, the whole energy-saving strategy and the exact structural solution to the dome, as well as the placing of transparent panels in both skins, took time to find their final form.

In line with the original concept, the floors stop short of the dome and step back to create a perimeter of toplit reading areas edged by a continuous desk. To optimise the number of reading places, the desk, like the edge of the floor slab and the corresponding balustrade, follows a serpentine curve in plan to maximise its length. On each floor the swelling or receding curves are out of phase with those above and below, so creating contrasting areas of greater and lesser height below translucent ceiling or concrete slab, and thus a choice of conditions as well as formal and spatial animation.

Rising from the basement through all floors, and widening as it does so, is a central well that contains

Left above and below: Details of the 1:50 sketch model made by the design team. During the course of the project, this model formed the backdrop for design meetings in the Berlin office and was gradually modified as design details were resolved.

Right: Models were a key tool in developing the design. This sketch model allowed the team to test the configuration of the perimeter desking and its relationship with the bookstacks.

the main stair. The upper floors cut back towards this well, making the stair immediately visible and aiding orientation, as well as framing the ground floor control and information counter and emphasising the building's symmetry. This slot also further elongates the perimeter worktop, creating workstations with commanding views of the entrance and its comings and goings. Flanking the central well are two service cores containing toilets and escape stairs, and the vertical ducts that play an essential role in ventilating the library.

The energy efficient control of the internal environment is achieved through a number of sub-systems that work together. Moreover, they do so in a variety of ways as, depending on conditions outside, each sub-system changes its mode of operation under the command of the computerised building management system (BMS). Indeed, for such a low-cost building the range of these systems and the way they interact is very sophisticated, achieving energy savings of 35 per cent in comparison with other recent library buildings in Berlin.

As usual, the key to understanding it all lies in the cross-section, in which each element plays its role. The heavy concrete floor slabs have a high thermal inertia and smooth out fluctuations in temperatures. Pipes run within these slabs and during the extremes of summer and winter they can be cooled or warmed by chilled or hot water from a district system. Below the basement slab is a plenum, into which fresh cool air is admitted through opening panels around the perimeter, and from which air rises through the floor slab above and up the ventilation shafts.

Besides admitting abundant natural light the dome also plays key roles in ventilating the building. The outer shell consists of silver pvf2-coated insulated aluminium panels, punctuated by double-glazed units. The latter make up 30 per cent of the surface and are placed, after extensive computer study, to allow optimum light inside while restricting direct sunlight. Both opaque and glazed panels around the lower parts of the dome and some at the top of it can flap open, operated by electric motors under the control of the BMS, allowing air to enter or escape.

The inner skin is made of panels of white translucent glass fibre fabric. Into some of these are inserted clear sheets of ETFE (ethylene tetrafluoroethylene) allowing views outside and glimpses of the structure between the skins. This inner skin both allows air to pass through it and, together with the outer skin, forms a cavity through which air rises by stack effect. Some glazed panels

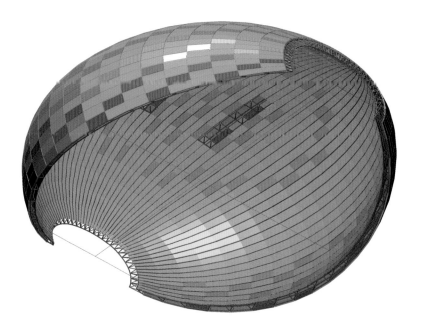

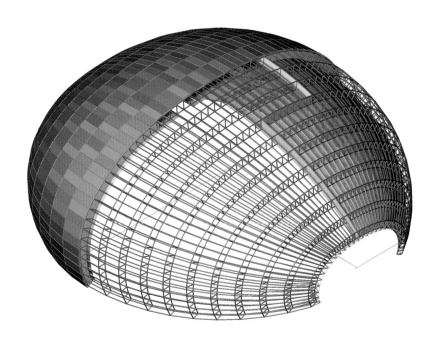

Above: Using computer modelling, it was possible to study light penetration through the cladding at different times of the day. This drawing is just one of numerous such studies.

Left: Computer model showing the MERO structural frame with the interior and exterior cladding stripped back.

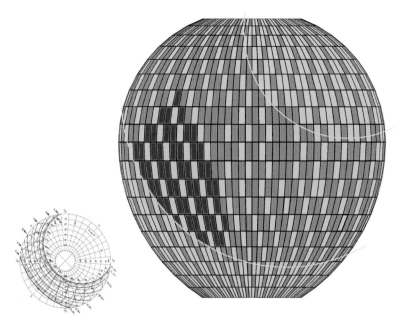

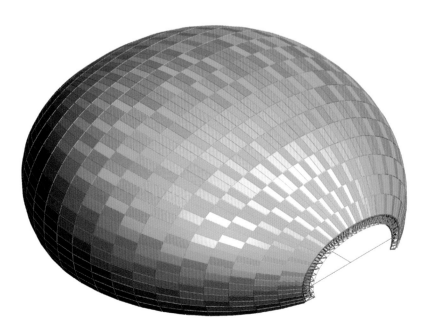

Above: This sun path diagram shows the pattern of solid and open roof panels. The design aims to strike a balance between an evenly day-lit interior and allowing sunlight penetration at certain times of the day.

Left: An exterior computer daylight study, corresponding with the interior model opposite.

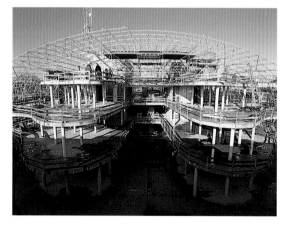

Top: The library's reinforced concrete floors seen under construction in August 2002.

Above: Beginning in October 2003, the MERO frame was craned into position in sections.

in the outer skin are positioned to let in early morning sunlight to start up this natural ventilation cycle while the sun through other glazed panels at the top of the dome reinforces air movement patterns.

In moderate temperatures the library is simply cross-ventilated through panels opened around its sides, the air movement driven by breezes or drawn by temperature differentials between the sunny and shaded sides. If this air movement is insufficient or temperatures increase, panels at the top of the dome open to exhaust air rising by stack effect through the cavity, replenishing fresh air being drawn in at ground level. Micro weather stations around the university warn if strong winds or rain are approaching, in which case the BMS shuts the panels. These same systems can be used at night to purge excessive heat absorbed by the concrete structure during the day.

Air cooled in the plenum is also admitted through the basement floor and drawn up the ventilation shafts to be admitted at each floor. Cool air might also be admitted from the shady side of the dome while warmed air is drawn into and up through the cavity to be exhausted at the top. In winter extremes the panels in the outer skin remain closed. But fresh air is drawn through fixed perforated panels into the plenum and warmed there before rising through the floor above

Left: A striking image of the
building site after a fresh
snowfall in February 2004.

or being drawn up the ventilation shafts. Further
warmed by floor slabs (in winter heating mode) this
air is drawn into the cavity and rises to the top of the
dome. From here it is drawn down again through other
ducts in the cores to a heat exchanger in the plenum
that recaptures the heat to warm incoming air before
the stale air is exhausted.

As these energy-saving strategies were being
devised and refined, various solutions were explored
for the structure of the dome. It was only at a relatively
late stage that a proprietary system was found that
could be adapted satisfactorily. Aptly enough, this
system dates from the same era as the original Free
University buildings when, partly under the influence
of Buckminster Fuller, there was great interest in
achieving large spans with lightweight triangulated
structures that dispersed loads in a number of
directions. The most common of these structures
is the space frame, and the most elegant of these
is the MERO system with tubular members tapering
to threaded ends that screw into spherical joints.

Originally this system was used only for horizontal
spans. Now, however, with the aid of advanced
computer programs, the system can be adapted to
suit almost any geometric form – even an ovoid dome
which, unlike a spherical dome, has very little repetition

in the lengths of its members. The panels of the
outer shell are set in a neoprene gasket system, also
manufactured by MERO. (The resultant building recalls
early Foster projects inspired by Fuller, such as the
Climatroffice, but the library is exactly tailored to
specific functions in a way the more generic space
of that earlier project was not.)

As if in remembrance of the era in which the
MERO system was developed, the structural frame
of the dome is painted a bright colour – an egg-yolk
yellow. When glimpsed through the clear panels in the
inner skin (or through the glazed panels of the outer
shell) the yellow provides an enlivening contrast with
the muted monochrome shades of grey and off-white
that pervade elsewhere. It is an especially welcome
presence on grey Berlin winter days. The funnel-like
element that connects the library with the old building
is also painted egg-yolk yellow inside and out, providing
a point of linkage in both senses.

The glazed entrance opening from the corridor
'street' is shaped to fit the end of this yellow joint
element. The resultant non-orthogonal geometry
signals immediately that the library introduces a
formal language very different to that of the existing
architecture. On entering, the visitor is presented
with a spectacle whose dynamism and drama is found

Right: The MERO frame relies
on a series of steel rods and
connecting spherical nodes, the
latter ranging from the size of a
tennis ball to that of a pumpkin.

Above: An aerial view of
the completed MERO frame,
seen before installation of
the cladding.

Right: The external cladding
comprises glazed and anodised
aluminium panels, secured in
a neoprene gasket system
also manufactured by MERO.

**In a playful allusion to the importance
of colour in the original campus, the
supporting steel frame – which is
formed of radial geometries – is
painted yellow, making the structure
legible and emphasising the cavity
between the inner and outer skins.**
GA Document, November 2005

Left: The bank of roof lights at the top of the building, shown in the open position to allow the maximum flow of air up through the library space.

nowhere else in the University. Straight ahead is the receding slot drawing attention to the control counter and the main stair while to either side the curved ends of the upper floors thrust forward. The fabric inner skin of the dome floats above all this, softly enveloping the space. The joints between the elongated panels tend to reinforce the longitudinal movement suggested by the slot as well as the overriding symmetry of the space, while the transparent panels give momentary views of structure and sky. On sunny days, shafts of sunlight cast shifting bright patches on the fabric ceiling that enliven and animate the space.

Moving forward into the library it becomes obvious that the dynamism and drama are in no way gratuitous but are a consequence of the clarity of organisation and the distilled attention to the building's functioning, both in terms of its human use and the workings of its environmental control systems. The building communicates at a glance where everything is and how it is to be used. Everything is in the right sequence: entry, control and information counters, main stair, bookstacks, reading areas and so on. The opening and closing of the panels in the outer shell even gives some inkling of how the ventilation system works. Everything seems satisfyingly apt and enjoyable to use, particularly the well-lit reading desks under the

intimate and bright-lit embrace of the fabric ceiling, or those desks with commanding views of the entrance, from where you can watch for friends and keep in touch with university life.

Each workspace is equipped with a reading light as well as power and Internet connections for laptops. There is even a hook to which to chain your laptop if you wish to leave for a while, a reversion to medieval precedent, although then it was the library books that were chained, not the reader's own property. Equally pleasant to use are the lounge-like areas on the upper level, where readers can curl up in easy chairs. Even the reading spaces around the perimeter of the basement, the only ones without an internal view or a glimpse outside, enjoy a certain dynamic drama from the natural light flooding down to them, and the space rising above.

Although the library is compact it is also relatively complex in form and everywhere there is evidence of the stringencies required to realise it on its tight budget. Concrete is unfinished or simply painted, sprinkler systems hang fully exposed below the concrete slabs, the bookshelves are a proprietary industrial system, and the ETFE panels are simply taped into the fibreglass fabric ceiling – an extraordinarily nonchalant detail. On the stair

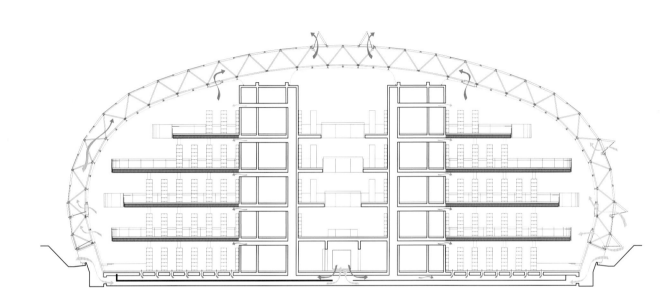

Above: Summer cooling. When the internal temperature is within the range from +16 to +24 degrees Celsius, cooling is provided by concrete tempering (chilled floors). Natural ventilation operates, with the outer skin flaps open as required. On peak summer days, which statistically are expected to occur eight to ten times a year, the outer skin flaps are closed and mechanical cooling is provided by existing compression coolers located in the original university building. There is no full air conditioning or humidity control.

and its landings, glass balustrades were unaffordable and so steel mesh is used, with handsome results. Here as elsewhere a virtue has been made of necessity. Details have been developed with a satisfying directness, specifically for and in character with the building. Sometimes, as here, a prime reason to admire a design is that a little has been made to go a long way.

A germinal concern of modern architecture was with the relationship of means and ends, with using limited resources to achieve a richness of functionality and choice, what Foster himself (echoing Buckminster Fuller) describes as doing 'more with less'. Hence the concern with abstractly stripped form and detail, and with repetitive industrialised components, which the computer can now customise, as with the library's space-frame structure. In its relationship of means to ends, the library is exemplary, proving the result need not be drably utilitarian nor dispiritingly abstract 'universal' space. Instead, as well as having a strong and appropriate character of its own, the resultant building might be aptly suggestive and symbolic in form. For obvious reasons the library has been nicknamed 'the Berlin Brain', even if that does not explain the cycling helmet that encases it. Functionally though, perhaps the whole university

should be likened to a brain with the library as merely a memory bank.

But to apply some mechanistic or electronic metaphor to the library, such as memory chip, would be inappropriate. It seems too organic for that, both in its form and in its occupants' subliminal awareness of its metabolism and respiration as panels silently flap open and shut. Narrow-minded contextualists might object that all this makes it a foreign body, an inappropriate intrusion within the university not only in its formal language but also as a self-contained and centred form within the egalitarian spread of the university, where every point not only looks much the same but is deemed of equal 'democratic' value.

On the other hand, the Free University represented the leading edge of architectural thinking of its time. In exploiting the leading edge of its own times – rendered very different by the arrival of the computer, which has made possible the customisation of the space frame and the management of environmental systems – the library exemplifies its own zeitgeist. It is thus more true to the spirit of the Free University and its original design than any overly literal contextualism, which would inevitably be too retrospective, could ever hope to be.

Above left: A detail of the ventilation flaps at the highest point of the roof, shown closed.

Above right: The opening ventilation flaps at lower level, shown fully extended.

What is interesting is the combination of active and passive technologies and how they interact – that's the real environmental story in this project. It means that the building uses a third less energy than the other libraries recently constructed in Berlin. David Nelson, of Foster + Partners, 2010

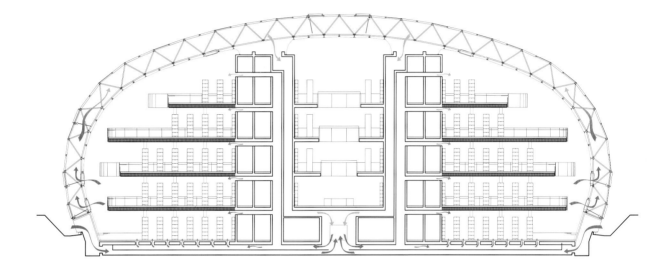

Above: Winter heating. When temperatures are in the range from +8 to +16 degrees Celsius, heating is provided by concrete tempering (heated floors). Natural ventilation operates, with the outer skin flaps open as required. When the internal temperature falls to +8 degrees Celsius, additional heating is provided by the university's district heating. The outer skin flaps remain closed and warm air in the cavity acts as thermal buffer. The inner skin flaps open to extract waste air, which is drawn through a heat recovery system. All these components are coordinated by an electronic Building Management System.

Overleaf: The library viewed from the green courtyard in which it stands.

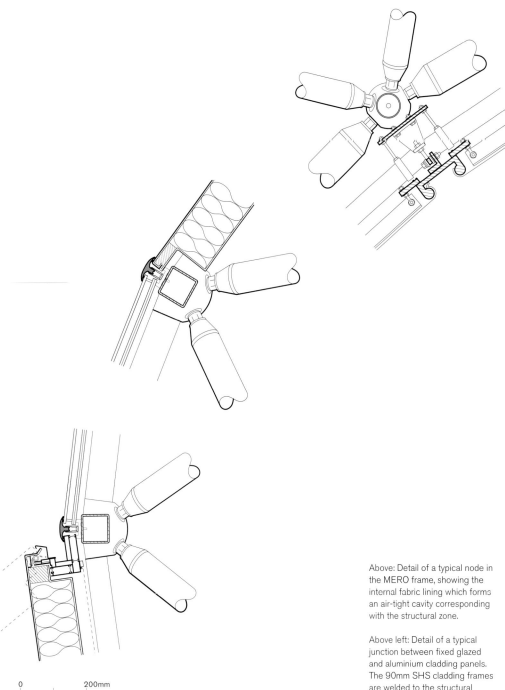

Above: Detail of a typical node in the MERO frame, showing the internal fabric lining which forms an air-tight cavity corresponding with the structural zone.

Above left: Detail of a typical junction between fixed glazed and aluminium cladding panels. The 90mm SHS cladding frames are welded to the structural nodes in the MERO frame.

Left: Detail showing an opening aluminium panel and the junction with a fixed glazed unit.

Right: Part section through the upper floors, structure and skin of the library.

0   200mm

0   6in

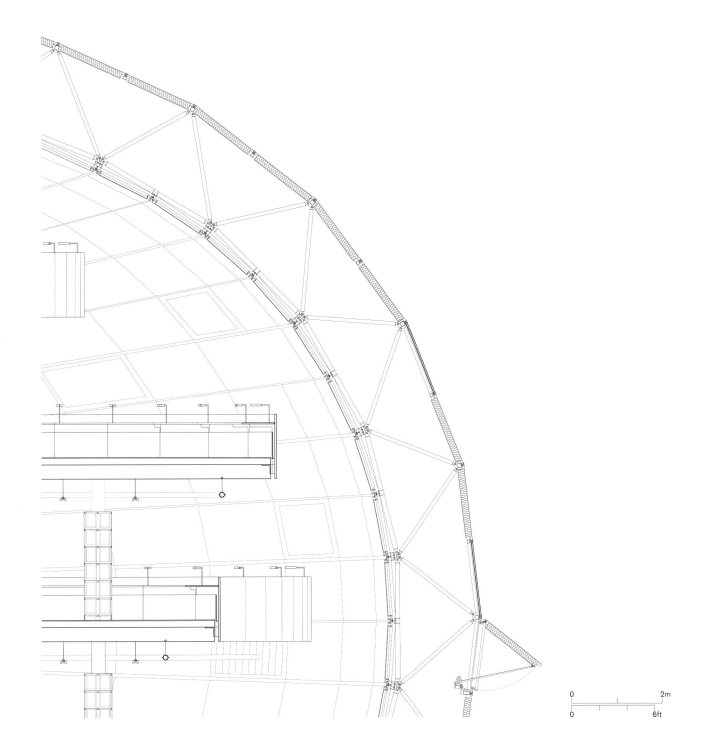

0 _____ 2m

0 _____ 6ft

The 'Berlin Brain' has been the library's nickname ever since the Free University president Peter Gaethgens – a physician – compared Foster's drawings of the building with a cerebrum. The metaphor is amazingly accurate. Ira Mazzoni, *Süddeutsche Zeitung*, 20 September 2005

A detail of the library's external skin; the cladding consists of panels of insulated polyester powder-coated aluminium and double-glazed units, sealed with neoprene gaskets.

Above: The ventilation flaps in the library's outer skin are seen here in the open position.

Right: The yellow MERO structural frame is glimpsed through the clear glazing panels that punctuate the facade.

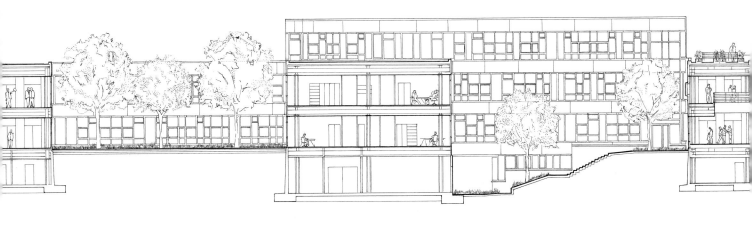

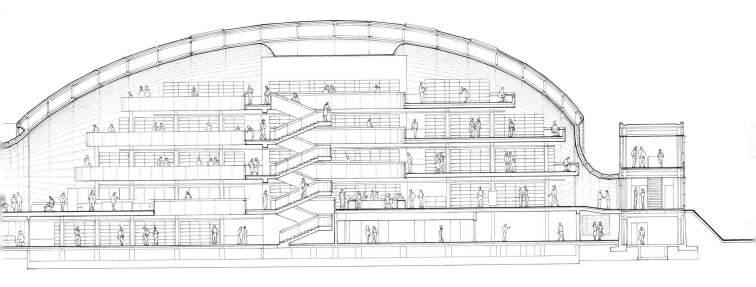

A longitudinal section through
the library's two entrances,
which connect to the university's
network of internal 'streets'.
Bookstacks are placed at the
centre of each of the building's
five floors, with reading desks
arranged around the perimeter.

The new building emerges from between the historic structures like a giant metallic bubble. Its powerful aspect combines the character of Richard Buckminster Fuller's geodesic domes with the latest advancements in sustainable structures. *Arquitectura Viva* 105, 2005

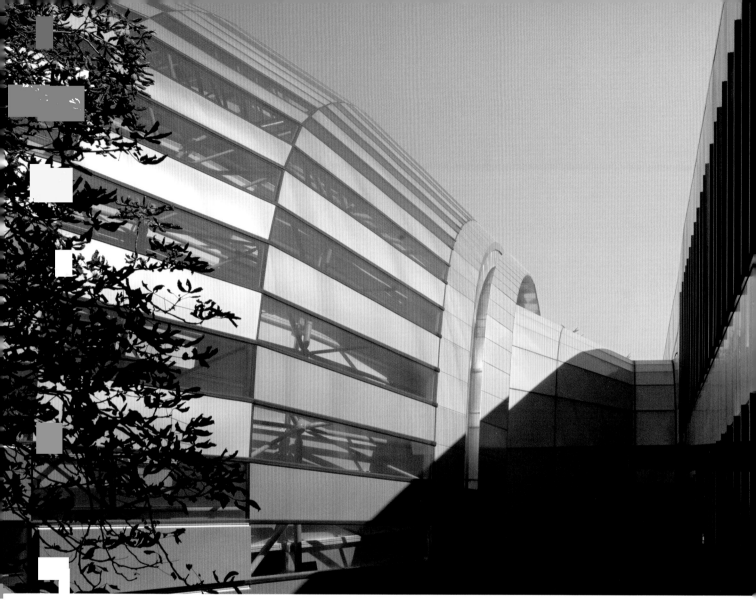

Left and above: Details of the
two connection points, where
the library 'plugs' into the existing
university buildings; the cladding
panels at these points are
painted the same yellow as
the structural frame.

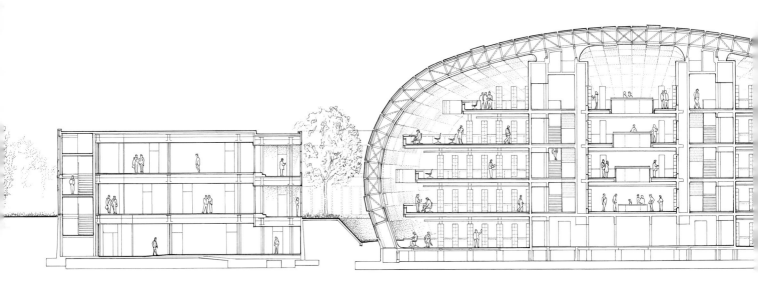

A cross-section through the
library and existing university
buildings, with one of the
auditoria seen right.

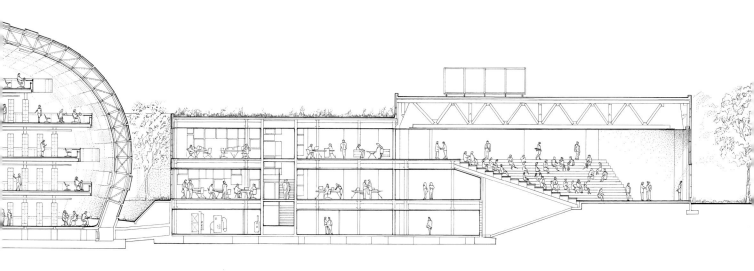

Above: Looking into the library from one of the internal 'streets' that form the primary circulation routes through the university.

Right: The view back down to the entrance from the upper level in the library.

The library works intuitively: the shelving is at the heart of the building and the desks on the perimeter, where you have light, views and privacy, but are still in close reach of a book. You could say it is an analogue building in a digital age. Norman Foster, 2010

Left and above: The edges of each floor follow serpentine curves, which have the effect of lengthening the edge condition, and thus maximising the space available for private study.

Within the library, a membrane of translucent glass fibre filters sunlight; scattered window openings cast kaleidoscopic patterns of light and shade that shift and change intensity throughout the day.

In the library, if you are reading and look up from your book, you notice how clouds move over the surface of the building because the light changes on that surface. It's a natural light projection screen. Stefan Behling, of Foster + Partners, 2010

The project was a quest to make spaces which have quality, which have an identity, which work in a friendly way that might lift the spirits, which might give some special dimension to the workspace and how it can work responsibly, ecologically.
Norman Foster, 2010

Left and above: Transparent openings in the internal lining reveal elements of the bright yellow MERO structural frame and allow momentary views and glimpses of sunlight.

Above: Here the bank of roof lights at the top of the building is seen in the open position, allowing the maximum flow of air up through the library space.

Right: Looking up at the roof lights from the staircase in the central atrium.

Left and above: Moving around the fifth floor, where spaces for informal study are provided; easy chairs offer the perfect place to curl up with a book.

Overleaf: The library at night.

Facts and figures

Free University of Berlin

Berlin, Germany
1997–2005
Client
Senatsverwaltung
für Stadtentwicklung
Project Team
Norman Foster
David Nelson
Stefan Behling
Mark Braun
Christian Hallmann

Bettina Bauer
Stefan Baumgart
Florian Boxberg
Niels Brockenhuus-Schack
Stanley Fuls
Ulrich Goertz
Ulrich Hamann
Andre Heukamp
Wendelin Hinsch
Andreas Medinger
Lars Muller
Ingo Pott
Michael Richter
Jan Roth
Diana Schaffrannek
David Schröder
Mark Sutcliffe
Hugh Whitehead

Consultants
Structural Engineer: Pichler
Ingenieure
Mechanical Engineer: Schmidt
Reuter Partners
Planning Supervisor: Büro Noack,
Kappes + Scholtz
Cost Consultant: Höhler und Partner
Acoustic Engineer: Büro Moll
Building Physicist: Büro Langkau
Arnsberg
Facade Engineer: IFFT Karlotto
Schott
Principal Awards
2006 Berlin Architecture Award
2007 Deutsche Architekturpreis
2007 Contract World Award:
Second Prize, Education Category

Project chronology

1948   4 December: die Freie
Universität Berlin – the Free
University of Berlin – is founded
in West Berlin by students
and scholars

1963   August: work begins in Candilis-
Josic-Woods' studio in Paris
on the competition design for
the Free University campus
in Dahlem

1973   The first phase of the Candilis-
Josic-Woods campus – die
Rostlaube – is completed

1990   Asbestos pollution is detected
in the buildings

1997   A limited competition is held for
the restoration of die Rostlaube
buildings and the design of
a new library for the Faculty
of Philology

1998   Work begins on removing in
excess of 6,000 cubic metres of
asbestos-contaminated material
from the existing facades
and ceilings

1999   Work begins to replace 15,000
square metres of Corten steel
facade panels
September: the first of the new
bronze cladding elements arrives
on site

2000   Replacement of the cladding and
renovation of the existing lecture
halls are completed

2001	Construction of the library for the Faculty of Philology begins
2002	Core works on the library are completed, followed by a rigorous cost evaluation
2003	October: the first of the library's MERO space-frame elements is erected
2004	December: the library's external envelope is completed; the fit-out of the interiors begins
2005	Construction of the library is completed 14 September: the library is officially opened
2007	The renovation of the institutes is completed

Free University of Berlin

The foundation of the Freie Universität Berlin – the Free University of Berlin – in December 1948 marked the rebirth of liberal education in the city after the Second World War; its name reflects West Berlin's status as part of the free world, as opposed to the surrounding Soviet-occupied areas of the city.

The Free University is the largest of the three universities in Berlin and one of the leading research centres in Germany; research is focused on humanities and social sciences and on health and natural sciences.

In 2009, the QS World University Rankings placed the Free University first in Germany for Arts and Humanities, sixth best in Europe, and twenty-seventh in the world.

The Dahlem campus was designed by Candilis Josic Woods Schiedhelm; when the first phase was completed in 1973 it was hailed as a milestone in new university design.

The mat-like arrangement of the campus was designed to ensure that the buildings could be reconfigured as the university's needs dictated.

Buildings are clustered around a series of internal streets and corridors to encourage open communication, with the faculty and facilities decentralised across the university.

The original structure and facade were designed in collaboration with Jean Prouvé, following Le Corbusier's Modulor proportional system.

The facades were fabricated from Corten steel, which when used in the appropriate thickness generally has self-protecting corrosive characteristics.

The rusty appearance of the original buildings led to the nickname of 'die Rostlaube' – the 'rust-bucket'

Vital statistics

The library occupies a site created by uniting six of the University's courtyards

The building encloses a net area of 6,290 square metres

Overall, the library enclosure measures 64 metres long, by 19 metres high and 55 metres wide

The library brings together 700,000 books from eleven formerly decentralised libraries

There are 636 reading positions arranged on five levels

The total building cost was 59.3 million Euros

Construction

The floors, columns and the two central circulation and services cores are of reinforced concrete

The external envelope is a double-layered skin with a wide-span MERO steel structure

The external shell is alternately clad in opaque aluminium and transparent glazed panels that correspond to the solar path, helping to regulate the internal temperature

The internal skin is made of glass-fibre stretched fabric panels with translucent ETFE elements

Energy summary

The building is completely enclosed by a double skin and double floor, which act both as air duct and thermal buffer

The mass of the building is used for either heating or cooling by means of concrete tempering

Heated or chilled water is circulated in pipes embedded in the floor structure

Flaps on the outer skin can either be opened or closed depending on the outside temperature

When it is very warm or very cold, the flaps are closed; during more moderate temperatures the flaps are opened to allow natural ventilation

Natural ventilation is used for 60 per cent of the year

There is no requirement for full air-conditioning or humidity control

The environmental control systems allow a maximum internal temperature of +25 degrees Celsius on peak summer days, of which there are statistically eight to ten each year

Heating is provided by the University's district heating system

All the building's temperature control systems are co-ordinated by an electronic Building Management System (BMS)

Overall, the building consumes 35 per cent less energy than a comparable modern library in Berlin

Winter and summer environmental scenarios

1: External temperature is below +8 degrees Celsius

The outer-skin flaps are closed; warm air in the skin cavity acts as thermal buffer

Ventilation is operated with pre-heated air intake

Concrete-tempering is switched to heating mode

The inner-skin flaps are opened to extract waste air; heat recuperation is activated

2: External temperatures range from +8 to +16 degrees Celsius

Natural ventilation operates; the outer-skin flaps are open

Concrete-tempering remains switched to heating mode

Solar motor, chimney effect and the building's aerodynamic profile provide waste-air extraction

3: External temperatures range from +16 to +24 degrees Celsius

Natural ventilation operates; the outer-skin flaps open

Concrete-tempering is switched to cooling

Solar motor, chimney effect and the building's aerodynamic profile provide waste-air extraction

4: Peak days – external temperature exceeds +25 degrees Celsius

Support coolers are operated if the internal temperature rises above 27 degrees Celsius

The outer-skin flaps are closed; mechanical ventilation is operated

Concrete-tempering is switched to cooling

Credits

Editor: David Jenkins
Design: Thomas Manss
& Company; Thomas Manss,
Tom Featherby
Picture Research:
Gayle Mault, Lauren Catten
Proofreading: Julia Dawson,
Rebecca Roke
Production Supervision:
Martin Lee
Reproduction: DawkinsColour
Printed and bound in Italy
by Grafiche SiZ S.p.A.

The FSC®-certified paper
GardaMatt has been supplied
by Cartiere del Garda S.p.A., Italy

Picture credits

Photographs
Archiv Manfred Schiedhelm,
Berlin: 15, 17, 21 (top left)
Richard Davies: 48 (bottom left)
Foster + Partners: 30, 40, 41, 45
(top), 46, 47, 50, 51
Freie Universitaet Berlin,
Universitaetsarchiv, HSA, FUB:
Rektorat/Praesidialamt,
Aussenamt, Photosammlung
Aufnahme Reinhard Friedrich,
Berlin: 18, 19 (top), 21 (top right)
Reinhard Gorner: 6-7, 62-63, 68,
76, 86
Rudi Meisel: 23 (top left), 26, 27
(top), 54, 55, 56, 57, 60 (top left),
77, 78, 79, 80-81, 87
M Rochat, Archiv Krupp Stahlbau
Berlin: 20 (bottom)
Nigel Young/Foster + Partners:
23 (top right), 24-25, 27
(bottom), 28, 29, 34-35, 38-39,
42-43, 58, 60 (top right), 66-67,
69, 72, 73, 82, 83, 84, 85, 88-89,
94-95

Drawings and Sketches
Archiv Manfred Schiedhelm,
Berlin: 16
Candilis-Josic-Woods: 19
(bottom)
Stefan Behling: 45 (middle)
Norman Foster: 4-5
Foster + Partners: 20 (top), 22
(left, right), 31, 32, 33, 36, 37, 49,
52, 53, 59, 61, 64, 65, 70-71,
74-75
Gregory Gibbon: 12-13
Jan Kaplicky: 48 (top)
David Nelson: 45 (bottom), 48
(bottom right)
Jean Prouve: 22 (middle top,
middle bottom)

Every effort has been made
to contact copyright holders.
The publishers apologise for
any omissions which they will
be pleased to rectify at the
earliest opportunity.

Editor's Note

In editing this book I am
particularly grateful to Norman
Foster, Karl Kiem and Peter
Buchanan for their invaluable
contributions. I would also like
to thank Thomas Manss and Tom
Featherby for bringing the book
to life graphically; Gayle Mault
and Lauren Catten, who mined
the office archive; Julia Dawson
and Rebecca Roke for
proofreading the text; Martin
Lee for coordinating production;
and the numerous people in the
Foster studio – past and present
– who helped piece together
the background to the project.

David Jenkins
London, May 2011